How to Deal
with
Toxic People

GREGORY L. JANTZ, PHD
WITH KEITH WALL

AspirePress

How to Deal with Toxic People
© 2021 Gregory L. Jantz
Published by Aspire Press
An imprint of Tyndale House Ministries
Carol Stream, Illinois
www.hendricksonrose.com

ISBN 978-162862-990-3

Printed in the United States of America
030622VP

Contents

The Tyranny of Toxic People

Toxic People.

This could be the title of a bad science fiction movie—a genetic experiment gone horribly wrong, or a planet-wide radiation leak from an orbiting government satellite turning millions of unsuspecting citizens into havoc-wreaking zombies.

If only it were that simple!

Compared to the real story—the one that lots of people live out every day because of a toxic person (or people) in their life—those fictional plotlines seem downright appealing. That's because in Hollywood scripts, a brilliant but unsung hero always finds the key to putting everyone right again and saving the world before the credits roll.

In real life, we won't get off so easy. The truth is, toxic people pose huge problems in nearly every social and professional setting: work, home, church, school, public places, private businesses, and relationships of every kind. NBC's *Today Show* surveyed more than 20,000 people to ask about their experience with toxic friends. An astounding 84 percent of women and 75 percent of men responded that they'd had a toxic friendship at some point in their lives.[1] And those numbers don't even include toxic coworkers, bosses, or family members.

The traits that qualify these people as "toxic" often become a significant drain on the mental and emotional well-being of others, sowing discord and dysfunction in every aspect of daily life. Is that a bit overstated and dramatic? I don't think so. Chances are, if you've ever had to live with a truly toxic person in your life, you don't think so either.

In the pages ahead, we'll examine the kind of behavior that defines a toxic person; the common origins of toxic traits; the ways in which a toxic person impacts the lives of others; and—most important of all—what you can do to protect yourself from toxic people.

A Moving Target

First, it's necessary to define precisely what we mean by the term *toxic people*—and that turns out to be trickier than it first appears. In fact, a hallmark of toxic behavior is that it frequently keeps one off balance through its inconsistency by:

- deftly deflecting blame or responsibility;

- playing on the goodwill or guilt of others; or

- outright "gaslighting"—making others feel as if *they* are the dysfunctional ones.

Often, the first step toward dealing effectively with a negative relationship in your life is simply gaining the confidence to call it what it is: toxic.

On the other hand, the term *toxic people* comes dangerously close to attaching judgment to individuals and not just the behaviors they exhibit. As we'll see, toxic traits are often rooted in past trauma or underlying mental disorders that cry out for treatment, not harsh condemnation. That is not a rationale for ignoring or enduring the effects of a toxic person in your life. It's simply a reminder to safeguard basic human value and dignity—even for the most challenging people among us—while at the same time learning to protect yourself.

With that in mind, here is a definition from *Psychology Today* that succeeds in preserving compassion while pulling no punches about the problems that toxic people can cause:

> "Toxic" is obviously not a formal psychological term but rather is descriptive of how people often feel when dealing with certain individuals. Toxic describes interactions where boundaries are often blurred, where individuals themselves and/or their behaviors are felt to be difficult, challenging, demanding, often adversarial. Toxic relationships are not fueled by mutual care and support but are often skewed to accommodate an individual's needs and demands. Needless to say, these are not healthy relationships and often, whether meaning to or not, toxic behaviors chip away at the equality of the participants and corrupt whatever could be good in a relationship.[2]

Another way to recognize you've got a problem is to notice how interaction with the toxic person makes you *feel*. No healthy relationship will cause you to feel:

- Physically or emotionally drained after spending time together.

- Reduced confidence in yourself or enjoyment of your life.

- Guilty for not doing more to solve their problems.

- Confused about your boundaries or beliefs.

- Frustrated that your needs, thoughts, and feelings don't matter.

Out *of the* Toxic Ooze

The good news that this book is meant to deliver is simple: *God wants you to be free!*

You have the right to choose healthy, fulfilling, mutually rewarding, and uplifting relationships, and to drastically limit or end those that don't measure up. It is not only possible to free yourself from the effects of toxic people in your life, it's *vital* that you do so to protect and promote your own well-being. An article in *Forbes* puts it like this:

IT IS NOT ONLY POSSIBLE TO FREE YOURSELF FROM THE EFFECTS OF TOXIC PEOPLE IN YOUR LIFE, IT'S VITAL.

Recent research from Friedrich Schiller University in Germany shows just how serious toxic people are. They found that exposure to stimuli that cause strong negative emotions—the same kind of exposure you get when dealing with toxic people—caused subjects' brains to have a massive stress response. Whether it's negativity, cruelty, the victim syndrome, or just plain craziness, toxic people drive your brain into a stressed-out state that should be avoided at all costs.[3]

Dealing with toxic people is never simple or easy, but I trust you have come to this book because you are ready to do what it takes to redraw your boundaries and reclaim your life. Read on to learn how.

CHAPTER ONE

The Many Types *of* Toxic People

Your boss takes full credit for a proposal you labored over for weeks and that represented your finest work. Your spouse belittles you in public, humiliating and infuriating you ... again. Your neighbor covers for your teenager who had a run-in with the law because she "knew you would overreact." Your mother calls to "offer support," but leaves you feeling criticized and controlled instead. Your friend posts unflattering photos of you on social media "because they're funny." Not funny to you, though.

Do any of these scenarios sound familiar to you? If so, you are in the grips of a toxic person. Call them by any other name—crazy-makers, troublemakers, instigators—these people know how to poison situations and relationships, stirring up discord and disarray.

Toxic people come in a wide variety of forms and degrees of severity. Some are mildly irritating while others are extremely abusive. It would be impossible to describe all types of toxic people, but let's look at the most common among them. You will surely recognize qualities and behaviors that you have, unfortunately, encountered in your own life.

The Deceiver

Lies destroy a crucial component of any relationship: trust. Once you catch a whiff of deceit in the air, look out! Sure, it could be an isolated incident or a half-truth that might be forgiven and forgotten. But usually it's a sign of trouble.

IF SOMEONE IS WILLING TO LIE TO YOU ONCE, HE OR SHE IS LIKELY TO DO IT AGAIN.

A person's need to lie is a telling clue about his or her character and emotional health. It may indicate serious insecurity, lack of integrity, or flimsy moral standards. If dishonesty shows up in a relationship once, it will likely show up again. Here's a sobering fact of life: If someone is willing to lie to you once, he or she is likely to do it again. People willing to lie in one situation or with one person will find it easy to lie in other contexts. A person who "shades the truth" with others will be inclined to be dishonest with you as well.

A lie rarely appears out of nowhere. It's part of a larger deceptive context. If someone is dishonest, you'll naturally wonder about the ulterior motives. If you feel closed out to certain aspects of a person's life, you have to wonder what's behind those sealed off areas.

> "WHOEVER CAN BE TRUSTED WITH VERY LITTLE CAN ALSO BE TRUSTED WITH MUCH, AND WHOEVER IS DISHONEST WITH VERY LITTLE WILL ALSO BE DISHONEST WITH MUCH."
>
> –Luke 16:10

Secrets arouse suspicion—and often for good reason. A person who tells lies must work hard to keep track of what he has said, and to whom. When the details of a story don't add up or keep changing over time, it may be a sign that you're not getting the straight scoop.

Here's the truth about deceivers: they create mistrust, chaos, and uncertainty.

The Control Freak

When you hear the words *control freak*, you probably have the image of a specific person pop into your mind—a parent, boss, roommate, spouse, or friend. Whoever it is in your life, you bear the brunt of someone who is uptight, judgmental, and invasive.

These are the people who meddle in your business, tell you how to do things, and hold you to impossible standards. They are quick to point out your shortcomings and always have the right answer (allegedly). They always want to win the argument and have the last word. They know what's best for you and how you should do things differently.

Here are a few primary characteristics of these controllers:

- Even if you give the controller what he wants to make him happy, that doesn't mean the bossy behavior will subside. Playing along to get the person off your back rarely works.

- The controlling person may "like you" or praise you for doing what she wants, but that's much different from respecting you.

- Controllers drain your energy and undermine your sense of self-worth. With them, you must take extra measures to preserve your physical and emotional energy.

- Controllers want power, undue influence over you, and "permission" to bully you. When you give in to them, you give up peace of mind, independence, and self-respect.

Even as they are engaged in toxic, controlling behavior, they will often deny that control is their ultimate objective. Their words and behaviors are couched as wanting to be helpful or being "for your own good." But rarely is their conduct actually helpful or good for you.

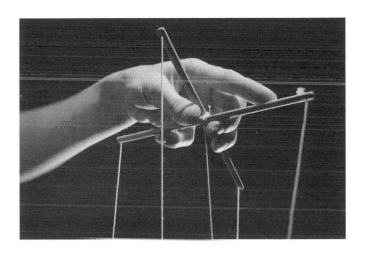

The Gaslighter

This person employs a form of psychological manipulation where he does or says things that cause you to doubt your own memory, perceptions, or judgment. The term *gaslighting* comes from the 1938 play and 1944 film *Gaslight*, in which a husband manipulates his wife into thinking she is mentally ill by dimming their gas-fueled lights and telling her that she is hallucinating.

Simply put, this manipulative person leaves you feeling that *you* are the crazy one. He will say things like, "Are you sure about that? You've never had a good memory." Or, "I don't know where you got that idea. That can't be right." Or, "That's what I'd expect from someone so narrow-minded."

THE GASLIGHTER LEAVES YOU FEELING THAT *YOU* ARE THE CRAZY ONE.

Through it all, this person is eerily adept at projecting a convincing aura of innocence or authority. It is as if he is a crazy-making Jedi, able to wave his hand and say the relationship equivalent of "These aren't the droids you're looking for." You doubt what you've just seen with your own eyes!

If you try taking this person to task for any of his underhanded ways, you might find yourself wondering how *you* could have been so wrong and so unfair. Beware if you are around someone and end up constantly second-guessing yourself, feeling the need to apologize, wondering if you're being too sensitive, or find yourself afraid to speak up for fear of saying something wrong.

The Angry Venter

Some people misunderstand the role of anger in their life, relationships, and interactions with others. They believe it is wrong to feel angry and that this emotion should be avoided or suppressed. But anger is, in fact, a God-given emotion, a natural and helpful response to frightening or unjust encounters. Anger can propel human beings toward noble goals, empowering us to stand up for what is right and to protect ourselves from threats to our safety.

> "FOOLS GIVE FULL VENT TO THEIR RAGE, BUT THE WISE BRING CALM IN THE END."
>
> –Proverbs 29:11

Scripture tells us, "Be angry, and yet do not sin" (Ephesians 4:26 NASB). Anger itself is not the problem, but the expression of it can be a big problem. Mismanagement of angry feelings and the inability to control heated emotions can quickly become destructive rather than constructive. There is a big difference between anger and aggression. Anger is a helpful physiological response to something that is wrong. Aggression is a harmful response to anger, lashing out in revenge and ridicule, sometimes escalating into verbal or physical abuse.

TREATING OTHERS AS VERBAL PUNCHING BAGS IS A CLASSIC SIGN OF TOXIC BEHAVIOR.

Angry venters have a pattern of heated, verbal rants that might also involve physical actions such as throwing objects or pounding a wall. Once started, these rants don't seem to diminish, gathering steam until other people in the vicinity become alarmed or frightened. Even harmless incidents can set off a venter, who is roiling inside like a volcano with the ongoing pressures of life. When those pressures are triggered, out spews a caustic tirade.

While many of us succumb to this kind of venting on rare occasions, anger becomes a venter's default setting, with his or her internal filter always viewing life as unfair, unreasonable, or unjust. When enraged, this person feels vindicated, powerful, and in control. She will angrily demand restitution from just about anyone, including those closest to her. In the rush of adrenaline, the venter may feel empowered and energized, which can become addictive. Treating others as verbal punching bags is a classic sign of toxic behavior.

The Know-It-All

This person believes he is right about everything, all of the time. It doesn't seem to matter what the topic of discussion is: how you rate a restaurant, the merits of the movie you just saw, or the news of the day. All of his pronouncements are correct and accurate. There is no room for a differing opinion or belief.

In addition to the know-it-all being annoying to be around, another oppressive dynamic comes into play: If this person is always *right*, then you must be *wrong*. While people are entitled to their opinions and free to express them, healthy relationships allow for two people to be respected and affirmed, regardless of differing viewpoints. The know-it-all, however, feels in competition with others, always needing to win: a sibling who "one ups" another sibling; a parent who competes with a child; a supervisor who targets an employee. For some reason, competitiveness is triggered in the relationship when the know-it-all feels threatened by the other person.

Consistently interacting with someone who must always be right is extremely frustrating. If there's a difference of opinion and you're proven right, this person will shrug off that situation as if it's not really important. However, if you're proven wrong, you hear about it often. Because of the difficulty of dealing with someone who is always right, you may disregard your own decisions and give in to whatever the other person wants. When that happens, you open yourself up to mistreatment.

The apostle Paul had something to say to know-it-all types: "Do not think of yourself more highly than you ought, but rather think of yourself with sober judgment, in accordance with the faith God has distributed to each of you" (Romans 12:3).

The Intimidator

"Get that report in today, or you might be unemployed!"

"If you don't play the game our way, you can just go away."

"If you don't do what I want, I'll leave."

The intimidator asserts control by issuing threats. This person is like the schoolyard bully who shoves a smaller kid against the wall and demands lunch money—"Or else!" Sometimes, the threats are issued at the top of their lungs and other times they are conveyed through a whisper or a look. Whether blatant or veiled, the threat is understood. This is the type of person the psalmist spoke of: "His mouth is full of lies and threats; trouble and evil are under his tongue" (Psalm 10:7). A person who threatens another always creates a toxic environment.

There are two main types of intimidators. The first is all bark and no bite. They deliver dire proclamations of what they are going to do but never get around to doing them. A classic example is the parent who says, "I'm going to count to three!" This is followed up by, "I mean it. You've got till the count of three!" This becomes a type of game, with the child refusing to obey just to see how long it's going to take to push the parent over the edge. The other type of intimidator means the words he says and backs them up with action. These are the types of people others fear. Whether expressed up-front or arrived at out of frustration, the consequences the intimidator metes out are always more severe than the situation warrants. This, in turn, breeds resentment, bitterness, and anger.

The Egotist

The motto for this person is, "It's all about me!" Egotists have an insatiable desire to demonstrate their own self-importance and enlist others to boost their self-esteem. With no need for humility, these people are most often described as prideful, arrogant, boastful, and conceited. Being self-centered is generally agreed to be an off-putting quality, but these people don't really care because they are, well, self-centered. Simply put, the egotist needs to look good, feel superior to others, and feed off other people's validation.

> "FOR WHERE YOU HAVE ENVY AND SELFISH AMBITION, THERE YOU FIND DISORDER AND EVERY EVIL PRACTICE."
>
> —James 3:16

If you're in a relationship with such a person, you have no trouble recognizing the signs of self-centeredness, including these:

The Egotist hogs the spotlight.

In theater, it's called *upstaging*. That's when an actor chooses his position to purposely obscure someone else from the audience. In a crowded room, the self-absorbed person will somehow always be the center of attention, sure to be seen and heard by as many others as possible. He will always adopt a posture of dominance; never deference.

THE EGOTIST WILL SOMEHOW ALWAYS BE THE CENTER OF ATTENTION.

The Egotist dominates conversation.

Self-absorbed people are unable to go very long without directing the conversation toward their favorite subject: themselves. Reveal that you've just returned from vacation in France, and she'll tell you all the reasons she hated it there—or loved it—without any apparent curiosity about your experiences or

opinions. Mention sports and you'll learn that he was once roommates with Peyton Manning's cousin, or that he could have played college ball himself, if not for that injury (or whatever). Egotists may nod politely for a short time while you talk, but they are waiting for the moment to jump in and start bragging again.

The Egotist disregards the needs of others.

Top priority are the egoist's needs, desires, and goals—not yours. This person will take advantage of you for the sake of his own agenda. A boss will ask you to work all weekend, knowing full well that you had other plans. A spouse will expect you to shoulder a disproportionate share of household chores so he can pursue his hobbies. A dating partner will make all the decisions without asking your opinion. Despite the egotist's lip service about caring and concern, you don't really matter to them.

The Drama Queen *or* Crisis King

See if this sounds familiar: someone phones you and begins breathlessly blurting out the latest dramatic details from his or her life, with all the urgency of a 911 call. There's been a nasty argument with the parents, a row with the roommate, a blow-up with the boss. The particulars of this latest crisis-de-jour aren't really the point. It's another "really big problem" to fume and fuss about, another calamity to fret over.

"It's all too much!" the person exclaims. "I can't take much more of this. My life is crashing down around me, and I'm on the verge of total meltdown." Again. Just like last week.

Got someone like that in your life? Someone who turns the most mundane situations into mayhem? Someone whose daily existence is one upheaval or explosion or emotional outburst after another? Someone with whom you spend a lot of time listening to their side of endless "dramas" and have the feeling it might be dangerous to offer a dissenting opinion? Call them drama queens or crisis kings—and call them a real challenge to deal with. They derive a sense of power from being at the center of an intense storm, and frequently whips one up when things get too quiet. They are known to orchestrate conflicts between people (including you) or insert themselves into ready-made ones.

The Put-Down Artist

You've heard the adage, "Sticks and stones can break my bones, but words will never hurt me." It's too bad that kids grow up repeating that phrase, because it's completely untrue. Words can be incredibly hurtful, as you know if you've spent much time around a put-down artist. These toxic people can be heard saying things like:

- Wife to husband: "If you were half the businessman my dad is, we wouldn't be in this financial mess."

- Teacher to student: "I had your sister in my class last year. Too bad you're nothing like her."

- Mother-in-law to daughter-in-law: "Jim dated some very smart girls before you. I'm not sure how you two ended up together."

- Sibling to sibling: "It's no wonder you didn't make the team. They only want people with talent."

A put-down artist uses words and tone of voice to degrade the value of another person. They seek to bring themselves up by pushing others down. The worse the put-down artist feels about him- or herself, the worse the verbal put-downs become. So the one giving the insult gets an ego boost, while the recipient gets dropped down a notch or two.

Sometimes a put-down artist uses sarcasm or biting humor to deliver harsh words. But rude comments couched as jokes have the same effect—they hurt. Humor can be an especially clever tactic because the offending individual sidesteps responsibility by saying, "It's just a joke! Don't be so sensitive." But inconsiderate or mean-spirited barbs, no matter how well disguised, still leave you feeling diminished and disparaged.

PUT-DOWN ARTISTS SEEK TO BRING THEMSELVES UP BY PUSHING OTHERS DOWN.

People who use words to demean others should take guidance from Scripture: "Do not let any unwholesome talk come out of your mouths, but only what is helpful for building others up according to their needs, that it may benefit those who listen" (Ephesians 4:29).

The Moral Authority

A "moral authority" person is someone who launches into sermons, regardless of the reason, using condemning language with religious themes. They use these lectures as a way to pontificate on the faults of another person, as well as the world in general. To them, even small mistakes have huge spiritual ramifications. The moral authority person is all about fire and brimstone—a religious Chicken Little, for whom the spiritual sky is always falling. Because God is invoked, taking exception to this person is like questioning God.

> "YOU, LORD, ARE FORGIVING AND GOOD, ABOUNDING IN LOVE TO ALL WHO CALL TO YOU ... A COMPASSIONATE AND GRACIOUS GOD, SLOW TO ANGER, ABOUNDING IN LOVE AND FAITHFULNESS."
>
> –Psalm 86:5, 15

Self-appointed authorities bring up God not to be instructive about his character or attributes, but to coerce compliance with what they want. When God is continually presented as a vengeful, arbitrary, condemning judge, the fullness of his love and mercy are withheld, along with forgiveness and grace. These individuals believe they are standing in God's place when they are really usurping it.

Mark could feel it coming. Depending upon how her day was going, it could be anywhere from five minutes to half an hour. If he could have forged her signature on the progress report, he would have, but she kept up with all the school stuff and knew a progress report was coming. Might as well get it over with.

Slouching over the counter wasn't an option when they were engaged in the "serious business" of his school progress, so he kept his back straight and his eyes straight ahead, waiting for her to read over the report. She'd read it over once and was going back over all the little comments. That wasn't a good sign. Mark figured she was gathering up ammunition to blast him. He wasn't wrong.

Mark had to give her credit; she could blast with the best of them. The positive information got passed over without a comment. Anything negative was proof-positive he wasn't trying hard enough. She even brought in his aging grandparents and how disappointed they would be with his mid-year science grade. They lived in Des Moines and he saw them twice a year.

Fifteen minutes later, the sermon was over. She'd laid out her case for condemnation and specified her conditions for redemption, which meant weeks of doing the things he hated more and things he enjoyed less. No progress report went unpunished, which seemed right since, according to her, he'd disappointed everyone possible, including God.

The Emotional Roller Coaster

Theme park roller coasters can be unbelievably exhilarating! As you're ratcheting up the incline, you wait in anticipation knowing that you'll soon be hurtled down and around and over and through. You also know that you'll arrive at the end safely, wind-blown, laughing, and catching your breath.

Roller coaster rides are fun and enjoyable; roller coaster people are *not*. That's because the emotional roller coaster person in your life is a constant bone-jarring, whiplash-inducing ride rocking you back and forth, up and down. These people are in continual motion of mood swings—high highs and low lows—often taking those around them on this not-so-thrilling ride.

Emotional regulation allows people to monitor their moods and moderate them, for their own benefit and the benefit of others. But roller-coaster people do not regulate their emotions. Some people are unable to manage their emotions due to physical conditions; others have psychological disorders—such as manic-depressive disorder—that make emotional regulation very challenging. Yet I have found that emotional roller-coaster people often make a choice not to regulate their feelings and moods. Generally, if they feel it, they express it, regardless of how that emotion affects others. The intensity and the unchecked nature of those emotions bring others on a wild ride that never seems to end.

The Pessimist

If you had to spend every day with one of the characters from A. A. Milne's Winnie-the-Pooh books, chances are that Eeyore would be at the bottom of your list. He's gloomy and pessimistic all the time. (Though in the Disney version, he's a much more lovable glum donkey.) If you spend time with people who have a "glass half empty" outlook on life, you know how they drag others down with them.

So why are some people persistently pessimistic? Life has a way of bringing headaches and heartaches that wear us down, causing some people to develop a cynical outlook on life. Many individuals experience disappointments and frustrations that challenge their ability to maintain a hopeful and sunny disposition. Other people, it seems, are born with a negative outlook on life, always assuming that things will go wrong and everyone is out to get them. Similarly, many people grew up in a household where skepticism and cynicism prevailed. These people carry that defeatist, downbeat attitude into adulthood.

Gloomy people create problems for themselves *and* the people they're around. By seeing life from a negative perspective, they invite complications and conflicts. They expect bad things to happen, and because of that expectation, that's often the outcome.

A pessimistic perspective is indeed poisonous to relationships and environments. In fact, research has shown that one person's dominant mood—positive or negative—transfers to others nearby, like a virus spreading. In an article titled "Does Pessimism Affect the Workplace?" journalist Lisa Mooney writes:

> One of the worst things about pessimism in the workplace is that it spreads. One negative-minded employee can cause others to quickly follow suit. When someone constantly speaks in a defeatist

manner, other employees can begin to speak in the same manner. Similarly, when a single worker behaves in a pessimistic way, such as only putting in the minimum effort on work tasks, this behavior can become contagious so that the entire production level of the company suffers.[4]

What is true in the workplace is true in many other contexts: homes, churches, schools, and community groups. If you are regularly in the presence of someone who spreads discontent and negativity, guard your heart and mind. Don't let another person's foul mood put you in a foul mood.

| *The* Guilter

For guilters, the most important person is the one they can blame, for anything and everything. Without a person to accuse, guilters would have to face responsibility for their own decisions and failures. Such a burden is viewed as too great, so another, more vulnerable, person is chosen to bear the guilt.

As they watch the other person strangle on all of that guilt, there can be a perverted sense of satisfaction. After all, they reason, "You're responsible for my pain so why shouldn't you feel pain yourself? If you are responsible for my pain, then I should have the right to tell you what and how much you need to do to make up for my pain."

True guilt is a God-given blessing, one meant to motivate changed behavior and elicit appropriate remorse for wrong actions. But guilters know nothing of true guilt because they avoid it themselves. Instead, they rely on false guilt, manufacturing whatever reasons are needed to keep the other person in-line and willing to accept the burden of guilt. Once weighted down with guilt, the other person is much easier to control. An Old Testament proverb speaks directly to this kind of person: "Acquitting the guilty and condemning the innocent— the LORD detests them both" (Proverbs 17:15).

When I first met Melissa, she couldn't have weighed more than eighty pounds. She was alarmingly thin from anorexia, her skin was waxy, and her pale face stark with protruding bones. At eighty pounds, Melissa was convinced she weighed much more. I soon came to learn that the extra weight Melissa was convinced she carried was guilt.

Melissa believed it was her fault that her mother gave up a promising dance career on the East Coast to get married. Her mother had gained fifty pounds while pregnant, and it was Melissa's fault she'd never been able to get it off. When Melissa's father left, it was her fault; the marriage had been fine before Melissa entered the picture. Having to care for Melissa meant that her mother never could realize her dream of establishing a dance studio. Instead, it was Melissa's fault that her mother's talent languished and went unrecognized—or so Melissa believed.

The blame for everything wrong with her mother's life was placed squarely on Melissa from an early age. In an odd way, Melissa's mother turned Melissa into a warped confidant, explaining in unfiltered detail how Melissa's birth had ruined her life. In a desperate attempt to make up for her sins, Melissa did everything she could to become a dancer herself. She became convinced losing more weight would gain her more talent.

By the time I met Melissa, she could barely walk up a set of stairs, let alone dance. Totally convinced of her worthlessness, Melissa assumed her mother's life would be so much better without her. The truth, unfortunately, was just the opposite. As a guilter, Melissa's mother needed Melissa. In fact, Melissa had become the most important person in her mother's world. Without Melissa, where would her mother place all her blame? Melissa had become the depository for her mother's resentment, bitterness, anger, and even envy.

Melissa's mother not only withheld emotional nourishment from her daughter, she demanded that Melissa feed her. Through anorexia, Melissa found a way to turn emotional starvation into physical starvation.

The Addict

Addicts are crazy-makers, raising a dust cloud of chaos and confusion wherever they go. People suffering from substance abuse disorders (or other types of addiction) will say and do nearly anything to cover their need and their actions. They will distort the truth and invent false realities. This often leaves others disoriented and unsure if maybe they themselves might be the ones with a problem.

Addicts anxiously plot out the next encounter with their addiction, fearful and unsure of either the certainty of each occurrence or its ultimate effectiveness. They live lives of uncertainty, which becomes subtly and overtly communicated to others. Friends and family members of addicts also live in uncertainty, unsure what the next crisis will be and what it will require. Those in a relationship with someone struggling with addiction end up struggling themselves, as their lives become entangled with the consequences of that addiction. An addiction is a devastating cyclone of traumatic events and behaviors that can uproot and unhinge relationships, causing damage well into the future.

To make matters even more difficult, it's often hard to detect when someone is in the grip of active addiction. That's because addicts are extremely skilled at covering up and hiding their problem, even from those they live with. You might convince yourself that you could tell if someone drinks too much or uses illicit drugs or gambles compulsively, but often you can't. Sometimes what you notice are the consequences of addictive behavior, such as erratic decisions, unreliability, irritability, dramatic mood swings, and dishonesty. You know something is not right—in fact, very wrong—but you might not understand what is going on. (Because addiction is such a complex issue, I recommend you read one of the resources on addiction listed at the back of this book.)

■ ■ ■

These descriptions of toxic people show the range of problems they can cause you. It's no wonder you feel vexed! And hopefully now you have a deeper understanding of how these individuals create troubles and how to identify toxic people in your life. Let's now turn our attention in Chapter Two to why difficult people got to be so challenging.

TELLTALE SIGNS OF A TOXIC PERSON

First the good news: The world is full of honest, kindhearted, well-adjusted people. Now the bad news: There are also plenty of people who manipulate, lie, and cheat. You can avoid lots of trouble by knowing what to look out for. Here are eleven warning signs of a toxic person.

1. **Truth-telling is not a high priority.**

   Even slight variations on what you know to be the truth, or careful omission of facts, is enough to put the person on your watch list.

2. **A lack of emotional intelligence.**

   This term parallels the well-known concept of intelligence quotient (IQ), highlighting the idea that emotional quotient (EQ) is essential for successful relationships. EQ qualities include the ability to manage emotions, connect with others using verbal and nonverbal communication, express empathy, use humor to deal with challenges, and resolve conflicts positively. Toxic people lack these vital skills.

3. **The person talks way too much and listens way too little.**

   Dominating the conversation often signals insecurity, self-centeredness, or narcissism.

4. **He or she always needs to be right.**

   No matter how big or small the topic, the toxic individual doesn't allow room for differing opinions and turns a discussion into a debate that must be won.

5. **There's constant drama.**

   Some people attract, and maybe need, consistent episodes of crisis, conflict, and clamor. They seem to thrive on having a big personal mess to clean up and feel uncomfortable with a calm routine.

6. **There are signs of addiction or dependency.**

   If left unaddressed, compulsive behavior involving alcohol, drugs, gambling, pornography, and other addictive things is sure to damage many aspects of the individual's life— including your relationship.

7. **Conversation is salted with sarcasm.**

   Derogatory comments and cutting humor, even if you aren't the target, signal a lack of empathy or a need to prove superiority.

8. The person has a victim mentality.

All of his or her problems are someone else's fault—unreasonable boss, unloving parents, lousy roommate, the government. Constant blame-shifting usually demonstrates a lack of personal responsibility.

9. Service workers are treated poorly.

Rude, insensitive behavior toward restaurant servers, dry-cleaners, and store clerks reveals an arrogant attitude.

10. His or her stories seem grandiose.

Exaggerations about accomplishments, acquaintances, and adventures demonstrate a need to brag, which is a sign of a shaky self-esteem.

11. The person tries to control you.

If you feel pressure to act and think according to someone else's wishes rather than your own, you're in the presence of a hazardous material zone.

CHAPTER TWO

Why Toxic People Are *That* Way

Barbara was afraid something was broken—in herself. In particular, she had begun to suspect that her capacity to get along with others was severely impaired, perhaps that she even had a mean-spirited, defensive streak that was starting to get out of control. As a Christian woman and a leader in her church community, this possibility was truly alarming. When I met her, Barbara wanted to know, "What's wrong with me?"

It didn't take long to discern an answer to that question: nothing at all, at least not where her current fears were concerned. The source of Barbara's distress wasn't a character flaw in herself. She was involved with a toxic person. Specifically, she was in a working relationship with a gifted gaslighter, which you will remember from

Chapter One is a person whose behavior is so well camouflaged that those in contact with them conclude they must be the crazy ones.

At her church, Barbara was a director of a program aimed at reaching out to the city's growing immigrant population. She was passionate about helping people adapt with language classes, free advice about how to navigate government regulations and processes, after school childcare, access to food banks, and so on. For her, the job had personal meaning, since she grew up in a missionary family and spent her high school years in a small town in rural Mexico.

"I remember what it felt like when I arrived in their country, not speaking the language and with no one to help me," she said. "And I go from there, helping people acclimate to a new culture."

After taking the job, Barbara quickly became overwhelmed by the amount of work required. So when Harlan showed up one day volunteering to help, she was overjoyed and relieved. He had recently retired from a career in the military and had "plenty of time on his hands." He made sure to let Barbara know he was available to assist her with "anything at all."

"At first I was so grateful to have an extra pair of hands," Barbara recalled. "But before long, I noticed that some of the joy I had initially felt in the job started to drain away. I wondered why, until I realized: Harlan rubbed me the wrong way nearly all the time, over silly little things that shouldn't have bothered me."

For instance, one day Barbara was talking with several immigrant children. She had learned to speak Spanish as a child and enjoyed being able to converse with the kids in their own language. That day, Harlan approached the group and, in front of everyone, handed Barbara a tattered book.

"I saw this in a used book shop and thought it would be very beneficial for you," he said. The kids giggled.

"It was a second-grade-level Spanish grammar book," Barbara told me. "I thought I spoke pretty well, but apparently not."

On another occasion he gave her a copy of a magazine article cautioning about the cross-cultural danger zone an American female enters when she talks in public with a Hispanic woman's husband.

"I know you'd want to do what you could to avoid making the ladies feel so uncomfortable," he told her, implying that some of the women had confided in him there was a problem and that he was on her side in solving it.

"With one thing like that after another, I was embarrassed or even horrified to think I'd been offending people without knowing it," Barbara explained.

She was on the verge of quitting the position she loved, mostly because she couldn't reconcile the intense anger and resentment she felt toward Harlan.

"It wasn't his fault. He was just trying to help," she said. "So why do I want to strangle him every time he walks through the door? I feel like my faith is being tested and I'm failing miserably!"

It took some time, but once she was able to see Harlan's toxic behavior for what it was and that she was not a "bad Christian" for how it made her feel, Barbara had another burning question: *Why?* Harlan subtly and probably subconsciously undermined Barbara almost daily, leaving her feeling incompetent in her role and afraid to make decisions. In his presence, she continually felt inferior and frustrated.

"Why on earth would he treat me like that?" she asked in exasperation.

| Ground Rules *and* Guidelines

That's a common response among people faced with toxic behavior—and in this section we'll go in search of some possible answers to that question. Before we start digging, however, it's important to put a few caveats in place, to help keep what we learn in proper perspective.

"Why?" has no single, definitive answer.

In a can-do culture like ours, we grow accustomed to the idea that every question has an answer and every problem an ultimate solution. Unsolvable mysteries make us uncomfortable. To utter the words "we don't know" is like waving a red cape in front of a determined bull. We assume it can only mean that we haven't yet invested enough time and research dollars to crack the code and shake down nature for its remaining secrets.

Yet the truth is, when it comes to understanding human behavior, so far we mostly have only statistical tendencies and probabilities, not scientifically verifiable reasons why people act as they do. To begin with, the number of conditioned and environmental variables to account for is astronomically large and their interactions mind-bendingly complex.

The bottom line is, why a toxic person does what he or she does is no more transparent than why anyone does anything. Why do you have a talent for music when no one else in your family does? Why do people love Shakespeare? Skydiving? Living off the grid in the woods? Thank God such traits have not yet been reduced to a handful of neurochemicals and well-mapped synaptic pathways! The magic and mystery in what makes us human are still mostly intact.

YOUR FREEDOM DOES NOT DEPEND ON CHANGING HOW TOXIC PEOPLE BEHAVE.

But where does that leave us in our quest to understand why toxic people behave as they do? Are we empty-handed? Not quite. In the pages ahead, in spite of this limitation, we'll identify several likely contributing factors to why toxic people are as they are.

But first, here are some things to keep in mind on our search.

"Why?" is a slippery slope that can trap you in "fix-it" mode.

As you will see in Chapter Three, there are many practical steps you can take to deal with a toxic person in your life, but "fixing" the person is not one of them. Most of us, especially in Christian communities, are conditioned to let compassion guide us in all our relationships. That remains a valid goal even when we're mired in a toxic situation. But the value of compassion lies not in helping you become a miracle worker, but in choosing wisely *how* to take action to protect yourself so that everyone's basic human dignity is preserved and your own behavior does not stray toward aggression or vindictiveness.

What the search for reasons *why* must not do is rope you into the idea that the person would change their ways—and your problem would be solved—"If only they could just ...." Consider this dynamic:

> Toxic people often make you want to fix them and their problems. They want you to feel sorry for them, and responsible for what happens to them. Yet their problems are never really solved, for once you've helped them with one crisis, there's inevitably another one. What they really want is your ongoing sympathy and support, and they will create one drama after another in order to get it. "Fixing" and "saving" them never works, especially since you probably care more about what happens to them than they do.[5]

As you'll read shortly, it's true that some toxic behavior may have its roots in underlying mental conditions that can and should be professionally treated. The key point to grasp here is that it's *their* path to potential recovery, not yours. Your freedom from the effects of toxic people does not, and cannot, depend on changing how they behave.

"Why?" is far less important than asking, "What now?"

It's important to guard against spending precious time and effort trying to "get to the bottom" of toxic behavior. At the end of the day, your job is to find the off-ramp in a toxic relationship so you can exit—or at least distance yourself from—a miserable and harmful situation. So consider the possibilities presented in this book, then move on to what must be done to establish healthy boundaries and restore your own sense of safety and freedom.

■ ■ ■

After reading these cautions, you might legitimately ask, "So why bother at all trying to know why toxic people are that way?" One reason is that "just because" is not a very satisfying answer. In spite of all these limitations, there really are some helpful explanations for toxic behavior. Knowing a person's motives is often a necessary first step in recognizing and naming toxic behavior for what it is—a *curable* drain on your mental and emotional well-being.

The Elusive Roots of Toxic Behavior

Now we're ready to unpack some possible explanations for why toxic people behave as they do.

1. They enjoy it.

We might as well start with the least comforting scenario—that there really are mean-spirited people in the world who take perverse pleasure in exercising the power to make your life miserable. They have developed a genius for knowing exactly where your buttons are and how to push them in the most disruptive way possible. Journalist Travis Bradberry calls this type of toxic person "The Twisted":

> There are certain toxic people who have bad intentions, deriving deep satisfaction from the pain and misery of others. They are either out to hurt you, to make you feel bad, or to get something from you; otherwise, they have no interest in you. The only good thing about this type is that you can spot their intentions quickly, which makes it that much faster to get them out of your life.[6]

It's true that a person who operates with this level of toxicity is easier to recognize than, say, a gaslighter like Harlan. But getting them out of your life faster can be another thing entirely.

Mitch was the highly successful CEO of a chain of auto parts stores his father founded in the 1960s. Under his leadership, the company had tripled in size and earnings in less than five years. He loved his work and took a lot of satisfaction in helping to grow the family business—and his own financial security along with it. There was just one problem.

"My sister-in-law is just plain evil," he told me. "I don't know how else to say it."

Mitch's brother Alex also worked for the company as director of marketing and sales. It's well known in business circles that family relationships often make for trouble in the workplace, but the two men operated well together in spite of the potential pitfalls. That is, when Alex's wife Lisa was not in the office.

"She doesn't even have an official job in the company, but just shows up unexpectedly all the time," Mitch lamented. "Then she proceeds to treat everyone like we're all convicts and she's the warden. She torments Alex worst of all, which makes him defensive and difficult as well."

Away from the office at family gatherings, Mitch explained, Lisa often yelled mercilessly at her kids, along with everyone else's; made cruel comments about others who were present, loudly enough to be heard; never lifted a finger to help with anything; and was always accompanied by two big dogs that seemed to have absorbed her snarling disposition. Mitch used the word *entitled* repeatedly when describing Lisa, who was the youngest of four girls from a well-to-do family. She attended a prestigious East Coast university, but left without finishing after being voted out of her sorority. Supported for years by her parents, she had never held a full-time job. When she married Alex, the monthly checks from her family stopped arriving, which "came as a rude shock to her," Mitch speculated.

One time, Mitch decided he'd had enough of her disruptive influence at the office, so he confronted her about her behavior.

"She looked me right in the eyes and said, 'All you need to know is that I'm a b----, and there is nothing you can do about it," Mitch recalled. "The words were shocking enough, but the look of pure pleasure on her face made me think she might be right. What can you do about someone who gets a thrill out of tormenting you and seems proud of the fact?"

Fortunately, there are answers to that question—and we are never simply at the mercy of someone who perversely gets a kick out of being abusive. Mitch and the rest of his family eventually developed an effective strategy for limiting the impact of Lisa's toxic influence—once they accepted that she actually took pleasure in their misery. That's the point: knowing what you're up against when dealing with someone who enjoys toxic behavior helps to clarify which path to take in your campaign to protect yourself.

2. Toxic behavior runs in their family.

When Erin chose to major in psychology in college, she had no idea her education would begin the moment she moved into her dorm room. Erin's roommate, Marsha, had already arrived and was settled in, like a dense, gray fog of pessimism.

"Before I even had a chance to unpack," Erin recalled, "Marsha informed me that the air conditioner was too cold, the cafeteria food was revolting, and the floor resident assistant was racist."

As the semester wore on, Erin started to dread putting her hand on the doorknob when returning to the room. If it was unlocked, then Marsha was inside, guaranteed to have an updated list of complaints to share.

"It was exhausting. I couldn't imagine how someone could get through the day with such a heavy load of negativity," Erin said. "Until the mid-term break came along."

That's when Marsha's mother and sister arrived for a visit. Erin quickly realized that family resemblance can encompass a lot more than physical traits and may include disposition as well. Upon their arrival—without even saying hello—the women unloaded about what a nightmare navigating the parking garage had been, how confusing the campus signage was, and how rude the boys in the elevator were.

"I think some people see the world as they do because that's the mold they grew up in," Erin offered. "Conditioning isn't everything, but it counts for a lot."

Choice and self-determination will always play the most powerful role in a person's life, but some toxic people may simply have taken the path of least resistance, conforming to the only behavioral model they've ever known.

3. They derive some "benefit" from toxic behavior.

Do an internet search of the phrase "types of toxic people" and you're sure to come across something like this: "Energy Vampire." It's a vivid term that describes someone who seems to feed on the energy of others, siphoning it away through negativity and drama. Somewhere along the way, these people become captured by the idea that — like a vampire — their survival needs can only be met at someone else's expense.

However, hijacked vitality is not the only need a toxic person seeks to meet through their behavior. Here are a few additional benefits (from their perspective) to be had from creating mental and emotional turmoil in others.

Safety and Control

Underlying the behavior of many toxic people is a deep sense of insecurity, the belief that the world is a hostile place always on the verge of overwhelming their grip on life. For them, fear of losing or being left behind is a constant companion. In response, they adopt the adage that "the best defense is a good offense." They seek to control the battlefield by sowing chaos and confusion in the enemy (you). It doesn't matter that no such adversarial relationship actually exists between you. So long as the toxic person perceives it that way, he or she will remain on high alert and act accordingly.

While everyone around them is off balance and uncertain, the toxic person feels the threat has been managed—never eliminated, but at least brought under control. Notice the war-like "divide and conquer" language in this description of toxic people, provided by psychiatrist Abigail Brenner:

> Their modus operandi includes gaining total control of a situation, and that means of you, too. They will demand your undivided attention and attempt to convince you that you need to join their camp. To their way of thinking they know better than you. They're right; you're wrong. And you need to do what they say. This kind of toxic person

will think nothing of invading your space and may try to isolate you from others you are close to.[7]

Understanding this motive for toxic behavior is very useful for crafting an appropriate response that doesn't waste time and effort on appeasement. Someone who feels threatened is unlikely to negotiate a settlement that gives you what you seek—lasting peace.

TOXIC PEOPLE BECOME CAPTURED BY THE IDEA THAT THEIR SURVIVAL NEEDS CAN ONLY BE MET AT SOMEONE ELSE'S EXPENSE.

Attention

Early childhood psychologists will tell you that, to a toddler, negative attention is often far preferable to being ignored. A toxic person is often deeply wounded, but has been unable for some reason to express their pain and take responsibility for how it affects them. They feel that no one listens or cares. Think again about the underlying fear and insecurity in the last point. Now imagine that instead of being aggressive or combative, the toxic

person adopts an attitude of victimhood, weakness, or neediness in order to accomplish the same goal. In other words, they use manipulated sympathy to keep the people around them from wising up and pushing back, or worse, abandoning them altogether.

Winning (By Any Means)

For a toxic person, winning is everything—which makes a fair contest unthinkable. Author Vanessa Van Edwards calls this person "The Tank":

> A tank crushes everything in its wake. A human tank is always right, doesn't take anyone else's feelings or ideas into account, and constantly puts themselves first. In a relationship, tanks are incredibly arrogant and see their personal opinions as facts. This is because they often think they are the smartest person in the room, so they see every conversation and person as a challenge that must be won over.[8]

That accurately describes many toxic people who are determined to win by sheer force. For some people, however, a better word might be *saboteur*, somebody who uses stealth and deception to make sure they come out on top in every situation.

Toxic people may have dozens of other more specific payoffs for their behavior—career advancement, vengeance for a perceived offense, monetary gain, and so on. The point is, so long as *they* think they gain from their behavior, you will continue to lose.

4. They never emerged from emotional adolescence.

Seasoned parents might look at some traits and behaviors common to toxic people—selfishness, making everything about themselves, addiction to drama, a tendency toward victimhood—and think, "That describes most teenagers!"

FOR A TOXIC PERSON, WINNING IS EVERYTHING.

Don't misunderstand me. I am not saying that being an adolescent makes you toxic. Why? Because we understand that these traits are developmental stages we all pass through on the road to maturity. We expect that kind of behavior and have mechanisms in place to help our kids emerge on the other side knowing how to choose and maintain healthy relationships.

For some reason, however, toxic adults never moved on from youthful immaturity. Traits that were tolerated when they were young hardened and persisted into adulthood, forming the basis for toxic behavior they never emerged from.

5. They are compensating for an underlying mental or emotional issue.

As we've seen, some toxic behavior can be the result of deep feelings of fear and insecurity. Now let's consider another state that may lie at the root of the problem: *pain.*

Life offers every single one of us plenty of challenges, traumas, and wounding experiences. But some people are further handicapped, either because the magnitude of their hardship is especially great, or they suffer from a reduced capacity to cope, for a variety of reasons.

Here are a few identifiable (and treatable) disorders that may offer some explanation for compensating behavior that is nonetheless toxic to others:

- Chronic depression and anxiety
- Personality disorders, including paranoia, schizophrenia, narcissism, obsessive-compulsive disorder, among others
- Disruptive mood dysregulation disorder
- Unresolved traumatic stress
- Addiction
- Hypersensitivity
- Insomnia

■ Unresolved emotional issues, such as anger, guilt, shame, fear

This book is not written for the benefit of toxic people, but for those of us who are affected by them in harmful ways. Therefore, this list is *not* meant to justify making excuses for the toxic person in your life, to inspire you to "fix" anything, or to complicate your own efforts to protect yourself. However, this perspective may inspire you to greater compassion as you choose *how* to go about drawing firmer boundaries— or possibly ending the relationship entirely. At the very least, understanding these conditions may help you avoid inflaming them further with your own responses.

> "OVER ALL THESE VIRTUES PUT ON LOVE, WHICH BINDS THEM ALL TOGETHER IN PERFECT UNITY."
> —Colossians 3:14

■ ■ ■

In her struggle with Harlan, Barbara finally realized something you may have observed about the list of causes for toxic behavior. In particular, her breakthrough came when she noticed what was clearly absent—that is, anything at all to do with herself. Nowhere among these "reasons why" does it say the toxic person in your life acts the way they do "because they are right about you" or "because you deserve it."

As Barbara told me, "Everything changed once it dawned on me that the biggest source of my distress was that I took it all so personally. I don't mean to say that Harlan changed, but his ability to get under my skin sure did!"

> "BUT TO YOU WHO ARE LISTENING I SAY: LOVE YOUR ENEMIES, DO GOOD TO THOSE WHO HATE YOU, BLESS THOSE WHO CURSE YOU, PRAY FOR THOSE WHO MISTREAT YOU."
>
> –Luke 6:27-28

Understanding that whatever drove Harlan to behave in a toxic way had nothing to do with her freed Barbara to embark on a two-pronged strategy. First, she went out of her way to be kind to him, offering compliments and positive feedback on his work every chance she got.

"That really wasn't for him, so much as for me," she said. "Jesus told me to pray for my enemies and bless those who persecute me, so that's what I knew I must do, because it reminded me why I was doing this work in the first place."

Second, Barbara started directing Harlan toward administrative tasks that involved little contact with the clients of the program or other volunteers. Soon he was spending less and less time at the center, and then stopped coming at all. In the process, Barbara learned an important lesson: "If you deny a toxic person the payoff they receive by mistreating you, it often takes all the fun out of it for them and they might just move on."

God alone can truly know the secrets of a person's heart and mind. We search for insight ourselves in order to better claim his plan for us—a happy, healthy, abundant life, wonderfully free from anything or anyone that might seek to rob us of that gift.

TEN SIGNS YOU'RE BEING MANIPULATED

The trouble with manipulative people is that they are typically very skilled at coercion and deception. To know if you're in the presence of a manipulator, you must be a keen observer of behavior and know the signs.

1. **You're always the one who is "wrong."**

   In your discussions—and especially your disagreements—somehow the other person ends up the "right one" and you the "wrong one."

2. **You get the silent treatment.**

   A manipulator uses silence to gain control and punish you for not doing things her way. If you ask the person the reason for the silence, she might deny that anything is wrong or tell you that you're being paranoid.

3. **You feel like a power struggle is underway, and your power is in short supply.**

   A manipulator needs to have control and superiority in a relationship, so you are not on equal footing.

4. **The person turns on the charm to gain some advantage.**

   Some people are naturally charming, but a manipulator deliberately uses charm to get something.

5. **The person acts like a martyr or victim.**

   When you ask for a favor or don't comply with a request, the person becomes melodramatic with the "poor me" routine.

6. **You are sent on frequent guilt trips.**

   You often feel guilty but in fact you have nothing to feel guilty about.

7. **It's implied (or said) that you're selfish when you don't submit or agree.**

   They'll turn the tables and try to make *you* out to be the self-absorbed one when you don't go along with their wishes.

8. **The individual denies culpability.**

   When you suggest that the person is not shooting straight with you, he'll say, "Me? No way! I'm not a game-player"— even as he continues game-playing.

9. **Manipulators minimize your problems or concerns.**

   Don't expect much sympathy or help from them for the issues you're dealing with.

10. **The person will frequently withhold.**

    They withhold information, affection, and compliments, while healthy people give these freely. Beware if you feel like you're never getting the full story or if you have to perform well enough to earn affirmation.

CHAPTER THREE

Break Free *from the* Trap *of* Toxic People

Relationships bring us joy and fulfillment like nothing else in life.

Relationships also bring us challenges and complications like nothing else in life.

You know these two statements ring true because I'm sure you have some loving, caring relationships in your life. And you have at least one troublesome, trying relationship in your life too—or else you would not have picked up this book.

I firmly believe that you can achieve healthy, harmonious relationships with the toxic people in your life. If you choose to make the investment—with patience, persistence, and prayer—a strained relationship can indeed become respectful, supportive, and enjoyable.

But it's also important to be realistic about difficult relationships. It takes considerable effort and clear-eyed wisdom to achieve the improvement you desire. And sometimes, despite your best efforts, the toxic person will remain stubbornly problematic and unwilling to join you in trying to experience compatibility.

Let's explore ways you can assess your toxic relationship and pursue specific ways to deal effectively to change it.

Seek God's Guidance

This is the best place to start when dealing with any problem facing you: ask God to provide wisdom, supply strength, and facilitate healing. Scripture assures us that God's character centers on love, grace, and compassion—and no doubt he wants our relationships to center on these qualities as well.

> "ASK AND IT WILL BE GIVEN TO YOU; SEEK AND YOU WILL FIND; KNOCK AND THE DOOR WILL BE OPENED TO YOU."
>
> —Matthew 7:7

I encourage you to talk with God about the difficult situation you are in. Simply have a conversation with him to express your thoughts, feelings, and concerns. Imagine that you are sitting down with a trusted, caring friend. What would you tell your friend over a cup of tea today? Where it hurts? What's troubling you? Your disappointments? Would you ask some tough questions? About what you fear? What you want?

Heartfelt and honest conversation with God is yours for the having. When talking with God, you can ask for wisdom and guidance amid all your struggles. Everyone on earth could use divine direction and understanding in their daily lives—and this is especially true for those dealing with toxic relationships. Prayer is a powerful source of insight and inspiration as you pursue wellness.

Receiving guidance also is achieved by listening closely to what God has to tell you. Why bother to pray if you have no hope of receiving a reply? The truth is, God speaks all the time, and we would have no trouble hearing him if we open the ears of our hearts. As Proverb 18:15 tells us, "The heart of the discerning acquires knowledge, for the ears of the wise seek it out." Until you choose to believe that God will actually answer your questions and provide guidance, it's likely you'll frantically do all the talking and make no room for his reply. To avoid this unnecessary mistake, slow down, set aside time to be quiet, and extend your awareness. Listen and learn, because God wants what is best for you and your relationships.

Evaluate If *You* Should Hang In *or* Move On

One little sentence in Scripture delivers big wisdom when it comes to relationships. In the apostle Paul's letter to the church at Rome, he says, "If it is possible, as far as it depends on you, live at peace with everyone" (Romans 12:18). Paul's words tell us two very important things:

- We should do everything we can to be at peace with others. We can use our heart, mind, and spirit to ensure that our relationships are wholesome and healthy.

- Sometimes peace isn't possible, because the other person is not willing to cooperate, is consumed by selfishness, and does not share the same peaceful ambition as we do.

As such, you will inevitably have to ask if you want to remain in and repair the damaged relationship, or if it's wisest to end the relationship and move on. This will depend largely on the role of the toxic person in your life and how much you want to (or need to) stay in the relationship. If the toxic individual is a spouse and you feel committed to the marriage, then you will want to work hard to resolve problems. If your boss is the problem and you need to keep your job, then you will also be motivated to smooth out the bumps in the road. But if the troublesome person is a cousin you see twice a year, you might be less invested.

Sometimes resetting the relationship is the right choice; sometimes it's not. If you choose to stay in the relationship, the key to begin repairing the damage is making the decision to remain committed to the relationship and committed to the hard work necessary to improve it. Depending upon the type and severity of the toxic behavior, you might be justified in ending the relationship. In some extreme cases, the best course of action might be to sever ties (in situations involving abuse, for example). Answer these four questions to help you know what's right for you.

1. Does the toxic behavior involve physical or psychological abuse?

If the answer is yes, to any degree, you absolutely must protect yourself (and others) from potential future harm. You should seriously consider ending the relationship altogether. Threatening, manipulative, and abusive behavior is rarely an isolated event. Odds are good that abusive behavior will continue. (Please see the helpful resources at the end of this book, especially *Don't Call It Love: Breaking the Cycle of Relationship Dependency*, which focuses on romantic relationships but has principles that apply to everyone.)

2. Is the other person willing to take responsibility for his or her actions?

Taking responsibility is essential for rebuilding trust and maintaining respect. Toxic people are often blind to their harmful actions or unwilling to own them. They will frequently brush off their corrosive actions as "no big deal." Others blame-shift, acting as if the behavior was someone else's fault. Failure to take full responsibility leaves you questioning whether the other person is willing to change in the future.

3. Is the damage so severe that your relationship will forever be hampered?

Everyone will have a different answer to this question depending on their beliefs, background, and circumstances. It is important to be able to overcome problems and not be held back in the future.

4. Can you ever truly get along with this person again?

If you have been burned by a toxic person a few times, you might say, "I want nothing to do with him ever again!" That is a justifiable response. But when anger subsides and you work through your emotions, you can better evaluate if regained trust and fair treatment is in fact possible or impossible.

Aspire *to* Build Bridges—Not Blow Them Up

This is the lesson Barbara learned and put into powerful practice in the story you read in Chapter Two. As much as you're able, adopt an attitude of bridge building as opposed to attacking or retreating. A peacemaking attitude is much easier for everyone to deal with than a hostile, defensive one. Practice maintaining an attitude of love and acceptance. This doesn't mean you agree with the toxic person and put up with hurtful actions. It simply means you are choosing to respond in a certain, predetermined way. When you present your concerns with a door open to reconciliation, you'll find that the strained relationship might have a chance to be repaired.

Part of this process involves realizing that you may be the target of someone's anger but not the source of that anger. You may find yourself in the unpleasant position of being the proverbial straw that broke someone's back, or you might just be at the wrong place at the wrong time. Take responsibility only for your part. Avoid falling into the trap of accepting false guilt from others. It is not your place in life to absorb the anger of others, no matter how you've been treated in the past. Deflect what doesn't belong to you.

Realize also that even if someone has hurt you, that need not take away your personal happiness. You are in charge of your attitude and response. You have the ability to deal with and do your part to build bridges, which will help you experience inner peace and contentment (even if the toxic person can't). If the hurt was unintentional, ask yourself, *Why am I magnifying it by holding on to it?* If the hurt was intentional and forgiven, ask yourself, *If I have truly forgiven this person, then why am I still stuck in pain?* Then reassert yourself and determine to be happy and at peace. It's a choice you should reserve for yourself.

That is not to say this is an easy choice to make when you're entangled with someone determined to cause you misery. Try writing a personal mission statement that defines your standards, values, boundaries, and aspirations as a bridge-builder. Post it where you will see it often.

It's important to think of those who offend you and irritate you as ordinary human beings, not monsters. Every human act—even a damaging one—springs from a person's own toxic mix of anger, guilt, fear, and woundedness. We all act as we do because on some level we feel that we must, given our life circumstances. While this is not a rationale for excusing others' bad behavior, it is an exercise in learning to walk in their shoes, see through their eyes, and hopefully find a reason for compassion. From there, it's much easier to contemplate forgiving them and moving forward.

Pursue Productive Discussions

Your desire to improve a toxic relationship will likely include an honest conversation about your struggles and wishes to make things better. You will need to talk about how the other person's actions are affecting you and how you envision a healthier relationship in the future. To ensure positive, productive discussions, include these strategies.

Have a vision.

Borrow a trick from great athletes and visualize your desired outcome for a tough conversation before you even begin. Reinforce the technique by creating a "vision board" ahead of time. These often consist of a collage of images you collect or create yourself that symbolize what it is you want. Like with your mission statement, place it where it can be a constant source of inspiration. This will help you focus your talk on a solution and ultimately manifest a positive result. It might even be helpful to share your vision and intention with the other person at the outset so he or she understands that you ultimately want to find a resolution.

Use "I" statements.

One of the fastest ways to get people on the defensive in a conversation is to verbally point your finger by saying, "you." Instead, try to frame all of your statements with the word "I." This allows the other person to understand that you are merely stating your perspective.

YOU	I
"You always …"	"When I …"
"You never …"	"I feel …"
"You should have known …"	"My concern is …"

Ask questions first.

Seek to truly understand the other person's perspective by asking thoughtful questions. If you don't understand what is being said or their motive, ask for clarification. Sometimes it's helpful to restate what you heard the other person say to ensure that you interpreted their words correctly. After he or she finishes speaking, follow up with, "What I hear you saying is …."

Listen actively.

Just because your ears are open doesn't mean you are listening to what the other person is saying. Hone your listening skills by staying present, making eye contact, and not interrupting. Also, avoid getting distracted by planning your response or finding fault in what the other person is saying while he or she is still talking.

Consider your tone.

Have you ever had someone tell you "I'm sorry," but know they didn't mean it? Even though their words communicated an apology, their tone sounded defiant and unapologetic. This is because the actual words you use account for only about 7 percent of how people interpret what you say, while tone counts for about 38 percent. That means your tone is about five times more important than what you say. So make sure you come across as genuine, regardless of what you have to say.

Be aware of body language.

So what makes up the other 55 percent of communication? You guessed it: body language. Our brains are wired to pick up on even the slightest nuances in nonverbal signaling. Not only should you learn to read other people's body language, you should become aware of your own nonverbal communication as well.

Focus on the behavior.

If you are delivering criticism, make sure to differentiate between criticism of a person and criticism of a behavior. Notice the difference between saying, "You are really negative," versus, "When you point out the flaws in other people, it makes me feel discouraged." Criticizing someone personally simply makes him or her defensive, whereas discussing someone's behavior gives the other person an opportunity to change.

Set *Your* Boundaries

Establishing a boundary is equivalent to drawing a line in the sand and saying, "You are not permitted to cross!" Or building a fence around your property and posting a sign that reads, "No trespassing!"

You need the emotional strength and clear conviction to know precisely what kind of toxic behavior you're willing to put up with and what you're not. To know what you want and what your boundaries are takes thoughtful self-examination. Carefully evaluate your situation, identifying times in which the toxic person crossed the line. Determine the limits you will set for yourself and the other person.

YOUR TONE IS ABOUT FIVE TIMES MORE IMPORTANT THAN WHAT YOU SAY.

Knowing your limits is great, but only if you can effectively let others know as well. It is surprisingly difficult for many people to verbalize what they want and need. Here are some tips for making that easier.

Keep it simple.

Make the effort to boil down the key points of your boundaries to a single sentence or phrase. This helps you crystallize and clarify what you want in precise terms—and makes it easier for others to digest it as well. Try creating two lists: one for the items that you *must have* in your life and relationships, and another for those things that you *cannot abide*. Examples include:

- "I *must* know that my feelings matter."

- "I *cannot abide* dishonesty of any kind."

Write it down.

Part of the problem with tough conversations is that few of us are skilled at thinking on our feet. It all sounds great in our heads, but as soon as we start speaking, the words get tangled. One unexpected question from the other person is enough to derail the train entirely. Making a list of talking points in advance, when you can choose your words carefully and be precise with what you mean, will help keep your feet under you.

Choose the right time.

If either of you is tired, rushed, or stressed by other things, that's not the right time. Do what you must to be sure you are both at your best.

Set the stage.

Difficult discussions sometimes get off on the wrong foot because the other person feels taken off guard. Avoid this by scheduling a time to talk and letting the person know in advance what you want to discuss. This communicates that you consider the conversation to be much more than casual and gives everyone the chance to mentally prepare.

Stay calm.

If you've done the work of defining your boundaries in the previous step, then there is nothing for you to defend or justify. You are simply stating what is true for you, with no need for anyone else's approval or consent. With this in mind, you will be able to keep your cool if the other person grows tense.

If you pay attention to these fundamentals, then this vital conversation can become a template for better communication about all kinds of things as you rebuild your relationship.

| Hold *Your* Boundaries

You know what you want and need. You've let the other person know as well. Now comes the really tricky part: making sure those boundaries are respected and enforced. This is key to preventing future harm. How to do that is remarkably simple—but not necessarily easy. Here's how:

Be consistent.

Once you've communicated your boundaries, then it's up to you to avoid letting things slide. Mixed messages will undermine everything you've worked for so far.

Be firm.

People often fail to consistently enforce their own boundaries because they fail to understand the difference between assertiveness and aggression. We fear appearing pushy or combative. But clear, direct communication is perfectly reasonable behavior and necessary when it comes to holding your ground.

Be grateful.

Don't be afraid to acknowledge when someone succeeds in changing their behavior to accommodate your boundaries.

Develop Skills *to* Avoid Becoming a People-Pleaser

Toxic individuals are adept at recognizing and taking advantage of people who are eager to please. Make that *too eager* to please.

When you are emotionally healthy, you can choose how to respond to others. You can make choices you know will please the people in your life, you can take care of yourself with choices that may be unpopular with others, and you can even push back or confront when necessary.

But for someone who is a chronic people-pleaser, those choices can feel out of reach. People-pleasers often behave as if being compliant is the only real option. They can even convince themselves that it's the "right" or "selfless" thing to do. All the while, resentment can build below the surface.

If you feel like you are a people-pleaser, the following principles can help you steer toward a healthier, more balanced path.

Embrace the idea that healthy relationships are balanced.

If you're in a relationship where you do all the giving and the other person makes all the decisions, that's a huge red flag. The first step to balancing the relationships you're in (or finding healthier relationships) is to strengthen your understanding of what a healthy relationship really looks like.

One way to begin is to take inventory, to assess the balance of power in the relationship. Take out two sheets of paper, one for each of you. Now divide each page into two columns. Label the first, "Rights" and the second, "Responsibilities." Now begin filling them in. What rights do you feel you have in the relationship versus the toxic person? What responsibilities do you each have? It will quickly become apparent if the relationship is one-sided.

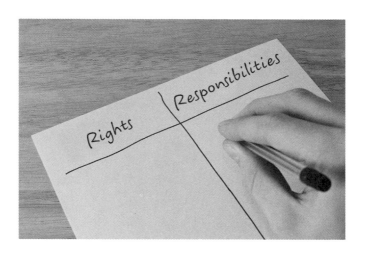

Nurture your confidence and self-worth.

People-pleasing is often rooted in low self-esteem. People-pleasers tend to feel insecure or may be convinced that they need to please others in order to be liked or even loved. Boost your confidence by:

- strengthening your friendships,

- pursuing adventure,

- practicing self-care activities, and

- prioritizing things that bring joy and meaning to your life.

Doing so will also remind you that pleasing yourself is just as important as pleasing others.

Rehearse speaking the truth.

People-pleasers struggle with speaking up and speaking honestly—especially if they think the truth will disappoint others. If needed, practice saying the words aloud by yourself or with a friend. Muster the courage to begin to speak truthful words to those around you. Do this regularly, and it will quickly become a new habit.

Stop thinking of boundaries as an attempt to control others.

If you define boundaries in this way, no wonder they seem pointless. But healthy boundaries aren't about trying to control what you *can't* change; they are about taking charge of what you *can* change. And what you can change is the truth you speak, the actions you take, and the requests you make.

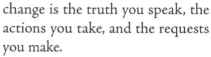

SPEAKING THE TRUTH DOESN'T SEND THE WORLD SPINNING OFF ITS AXIS.

Accept that being liked by everyone is impossible.

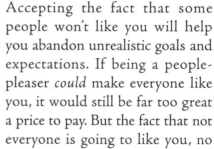

Accepting the fact that some people won't like you will help you abandon unrealistic goals and expectations. If being a people-pleaser *could* make everyone like you, it would still be far too great a price to pay. But the fact that not everyone is going to like you, no matter how compliant you are, makes people-pleasing an even more futile endeavor.

Act out of choice, not compulsion.

It's good to make choices, even sacrificial choices, to meet the needs of those around us. But saying *yes* should be a choice—and it is only a true choice when we give ourselves permission to respond in other ways as the need arises.

Develop new habits by practicing every day.

Start by saying *no* or expressing a different opinion on small things. You may find what many recovering-people-pleasers have discovered: speaking the truth doesn't send the world spinning off its axis. In fact, you may be delighted to learn that your loved ones and true friends actually appreciate seeing and knowing the real you.

> "THEREFORE EACH OF YOU MUST PUT OFF FALSEHOOD AND SPEAK TRUTHFULLY TO YOUR NEIGHBOR, FOR WE ARE ALL MEMBERS OF ONE BODY."
>
> –Ephesians 4:25

■ ■ ■

Here's a tip for helping you give up the people-pleasing habit: Make a list of all the good things you believe other people deserve in life—the very things you've made it your mission to provide if at all possible. These might include things like respect, prosperity, safety— you name it. Be as specific as possible, and keep going until you can't think of any more.

Now take out another piece of paper and write, "I deserve _____ because _____." Fill in the first blank with the first item from the other list—and complete the sentence with a powerful reason why you are also entitled to the good things you wish for others. Repeat until you've exhausted your previous list.

GOOD THINGS THAT OTHER PEOPLE DESERVE:

GOOD THINGS THAT I DESERVE:

I deserve _____

    because _____

I deserve _____

    because _____

Choose *to* Live *a* Grace-Filled Life

Forgiveness is essential to living a grace-full life. God extends his grace to us, and he expects us to extend that grace to others.

When you live your life full of bitterness and unresolved anger, that life is full of stress: people must be constantly watched for the harm you know they will do; events must be meticulously controlled to avoid the pain you are certain will come. Under siege, you become a raw nerve of reaction, stressed out and defensive. Peace is so far away, you can't even see a glimmer of it on the horizon.

The only path to peace is forgiveness—turning bitterness into kindness and resentment into compassion. By doing so, you claim victory over your enemies by refusing to participate in the war. By claiming victory, you establish your own peace.

As you seek peace with the toxic people in your life, don't forget to look at yourself. Sometimes the person we have the hardest time forgiving is the one staring back at us in the mirror. When you fail to forgive yourself, you may spend a great deal of time and energy attempting to make up for your faults, mistakes, and misjudgments. When you are at war with yourself, you're not going to experience peace.

In order to forgive—either others or ourselves—we need to learn to live gracefully. We must stop withholding forgiveness until certain conditions are met. We must stop demanding payment for forgiveness and instead offer it as a gift, just as God does.

I've heard more than one person tell me that forgiveness goes against their nature. Which nature? Children have an incredible capacity to forgive. Somewhere along the line, we can lose that capacity as adults, but that doesn't mean we never had it or can't get it back. Living grace-full means reconnecting with that capacity of forgiveness.

SOMETIMES THE PERSON WE HAVE THE HARDEST TIME FORGIVING IS THE ONE STARING BACK AT US IN THE MIRROR.

According to the calculus of this world, forgiveness—and the grace that it takes—doesn't add up. There are times when extending grace through forgiveness will be the exact opposite of what you feel like doing. Forgiveness seems risky and wrong. Grace sets up its own internal contradiction because grace is not a human concept; grace is a divine concept. Author Philip Yancey says, "Grace sounds a startling note of contradiction, of liberation, and every day I must pray anew for the ability to hear its message."[9]

No one said treating others with grace is going to be easy. Yancey continues, "God took a great risk by announcing forgiveness in advance, and the scandal of grace involves a transfer of that risk to us."[10] Living grace-full means living risky and at peace with the risk. How can risk coexist with peace? When God is in charge of the equation, that's when.

Sometimes it is helpful to create a ritual to help visualize the act of letting go and forgiving. Write down a description of the offense or toxic behavior that you'd like to forgive. You might include drawings that represent your anger or pain. Imagine that the words and images actually contain all the emotion you've carried. Now comes the good part. Choose among any number of ways to get rid of the representation you've created. Bury it, burn it, put it on the altar at church, place it in a moving stream and watch it disappear with the current; you are limited only by your imagination. Whatever you choose, visualize the burden of your

LIVING GRACE-FULL MEANS LIVING RISKY AND AT PEACE WITH THE RISK.

pain vanishing along with it, into God's hands where it belongs.

Don't stress about how all of this grace and forgiveness and risk and peace is going to work. Trust God to figure it out for you. Ask him to show you the way to give grace and forgive; then follow where he leads.

Focus *on* Healthy Problem-Solving.

Over the course of my practice, I've developed a list of characteristics of healthy problem-solvers. Problems, of course, carry with them the seeds of both consensus and conflict. Those who have grown weary of a toxic person can have difficulty dealing with problems because of the potential for conflict. Either they refuse to stand their ground and give in, or they turn every conflict into a do-or-die battleground of "this time I'll win!"

There is a middle ground between these two extremes. Granted, this middle ground takes more time to accomplish, but it has the best chance of allowing both people to remain standing at the end. Consider the following strategies.

■ **The goal is to resolve the problem, not to win.**
   You may find, if you only want to win, that you've won the battle but lost the war. Problems and how

they are handled have short-term and long-term consequences. Be aware of both.

Some problems won't go away on their own.
For problems that won't disappear, face them instead of avoiding them. As soon as possible, find a way to deal with them. Unattended problems can balloon out of control and are harder to address later on.

Be open to unique solutions.
You might have an initial idea of how to solve a problem, but sometimes, once you hear different opinions, you might change your mind. You may have a *good* solution at first, but it may not be the *best* solution.

Forgive yourself and others.
When the boundaries are breached, repair them with forgiveness.

Accept that life is not always fair.
Problems, and the way people handle them, are not always fair. What is fair to one person may be seen as unfair by another.

Deal with one problem at a time.
There may be other problems swirling around you, but you can realistically only handle one at a time. Don't try to take on all the problems of the world at once. They will bury you.

■ **Anticipate a positive outcome.** When you enter into problem-solving mode, be optimistic. This attitude may seem simplistic, but it is enormously helpful. If you begin to tackle a problem thinking that there is no good answer, how motivated will you be to solve it?

■ **Believe in your ability to solve the problem.** This concept goes hand-in-hand with the previous one. There is a difference in believing *there is no answer* and believing *you have no answer—yet*. Trust yourself to be able to find that answer.

■ **When working through problems, be aware of how you're communicating to yourself and to others.** Problems are stressful, so avoid autopilot problem-solving. Keep your head in the game and be aware of how all involved are dealing with the problem.

Reclaim *Your* Personal Power

Most often, toxic behavior is designed to convince you with words, actions, and ideas that you are powerless, without rights. This is a lie. You have rights and power. You have the right to be treated fairly and respectfully. You have the power to say *no* if someone threatens to hurt you. You have the right to live your life free of worry that you will be undermined. You have the power to forgive those who hurt you. You have a right to make your own decisions, even if those differ from the decisions of others.

Reclaiming your personal power means learning to love and trust yourself. All too often this begins at a much more fundamental level: *knowing* yourself. If you've been overshadowed by a toxic person, it may be that you've forgotten how to finish statements like these:

- I am _____.

- I love _____.

- I don't like _____.

- I want _____.

- I need _____.

Take some time now and complete those sentences as honestly and extravagantly as your heart desires. You may find it difficult at first, but keep at it until you've painted a clear picture of who you are.

RECLAIMING YOUR PERSONAL POWER MEANS LEARNING TO LOVE AND TRUST YOURSELF.

There was the man I worked with who went back to school and began a second career, realizing his first career had been his father's decision, not his own. There was the woman I knew who rearranged and redecorated her house, realizing she'd previously chosen items and colors her mother approved of, but she really didn't like. I've seen people adapt their religious beliefs, adjust their friendships, and alter their goals as statements of independence and reconnection with their personal power. In each case, they battled fear yet experienced exhilaration at connecting with themselves instead of trying to be or please someone else.

Still, reclaiming your personal power isn't just finding a way to say *yes* to the things you really want. It is also finding a way to say *no* to the things other people really want from or for you, even if those things are good. Many emotional abusers will try to force you into a black-and-white world of stark decisions, where their opinion is "great" and yours is "horrible." Many decisions in life aren't at the poles of great and horrible; they lie somewhere in between.

Ultimately, you are responsible for your own choices and actions. As the Bible says, "Each one should test their own actions. Then they can take pride in themselves alone, without comparing themselves to someone else, for each one should carry their own load" (Galatians 6:4–5).

FIFTEEN WAYS TO DEAL WITH CRITICISM

Being the target of criticism may be a fairly common experience, but it is also one of the most stinging. No one wants to be told they're doing something wrong, not living up to expectations, or failing to perform. To complicate matters, sometimes you're not sure if the criticism is constructive (meant to bring out your best) or destructive (meant to drag you down).

It's inevitable that you will receive criticism from your spouse, boss, or family member. So how can you respond in a way that will keep your self-respect intact and make the outcome positive?

1. **Consider the critic.**

   If the person is a family member you trust, you might be more receptive than, say, a coworker who is after your job. Recognizing the nature of your relationship with the other person will determine how seriously to take the criticism.

2. **Evaluate if the person is a chronic fault-finder or typically an encourager.**

   Some people have a critical spirit and a negative outlook. But the criticism of someone usually supportive is much easier to accept.

3. **Assess if there is an agenda at play.**

   Try to understand the other person's motivations. Is he truly trying to help you improve, or is he trying to embarrass you or make you feel inferior.

4. **Notice how the criticism was delivered.**

   Words spoken in a gentle, affirming manner indicate that the person is on your side, trying to help you improve.

5. **Remain open, even if you don't want to.**

   It's possible that the critical remark is accurate or contains at least some truth.

6. **Respond, don't react.**

   You might be tempted to give a knee-jerk reaction, defending yourself and lashing out to even the score. But hasty and emotion-fueled reactions will likely make the situation worse.

7. **Let the dust settle.**

   If you need a follow-up conversation about the criticism, give your emotions ample time to cool. Talk calmly and rationally.

8. **Evaluate your wisest approach.**

   Sometimes the best thing is to keep quiet and say as little as possible in response. Other times, it's best to ask for clarification or provide more information to clear up misunderstandings.

9. **Decide if you should own it or let it go.**

   As the saying goes, "When you're in the wrong, admit it. When you're in the right, be quiet."

10. **Determine what change is desired.**

    For example, if you are criticized for being chronically late, and you agree with the assessment, you know specifically what you need to improve: punctuality. But if critical remarks are vague, ask the person what exactly he is wanting you to change.

11. **Reframe the terms.**

    For obvious reasons the word *criticism* and even the words *constructive criticism* have negative implications. If you're sure the person's intent is to assist you, think of the discussion as *helpful feedback* or *useful input*.

12. Get a third opinion.

You know what the other person's opinion is and you know your own opinion. If you're unsure who's right, seek input from someone who can be objective.

13. Tell yourself the truth.

If the person's feedback proves to be right on, accept it without making excuses. Be grateful that someone was willing to be honest with you.

14. Ask for a positive comment.

If the person is willing to criticize you, she should be willing to compliment you as well. It's perfectly fine to say, "I accept your reproof, and I'd like to also hear what you think I'm doing well."

15. Practice self-acceptance.

Criticism, even if only partially accurate, reminds us that we're not perfect and have things to work on—just like everyone on earth. Give yourself plenty of grace and understanding.

You Don't Deserve Mistreatment

Toxic behavior from a toxic person often starts out as mildly irritating and progresses to become alarmingly offensive, or worse yet, abusive.

As a mental health professional for more than thirty years, I am very concerned about the often-overlooked issue of emotional abuse. For many years, I have noticed that the focus of abuse—even the concept of abuse—has centered around the physical or sexual aspects of abuse. The signs of emotional abuse, however, are easier to overlook. There is no scar tissue to stretch, no bruises to yellow and heal, no gaping wound to point to. In spite of their invisibility, emotional wounds comprise a damaging form of abuse.

Emotional abuse is often difficult to spot and easy to dismiss. But just as physical and sexual abuse have signposts to mark their presence, emotional abuse—being a systematic attack on one's sense of self—has common traits. Just as physical and sexual abuse come in degrees of severity, emotional abuse runs the gamut of intensity and damage. It exists, apart from physical or sexual abuse, as incredibly destructive to an emerging sense of self.

YOU DESERVE TO BE TREATED WITH RESPECT, HONOR, AND DIGNITY AT ALL TIMES, BY ALL PEOPLE.

All of us have, at one time or another, come under attack by people who just happen to be having a bad day. They take out their frustrations on us, and we feel battered by the winds of their emotions. We have all had it happen to us, and we have all probably been guilty of it a time or two. No one is perfect, and all of us slip up and occasionally say or do things we know we shouldn't. That's normal.

Emotional abuse isn't normal. Emotional abuse is the consistent pattern of being treated unfairly and unjustly over a period of time, usually by the same person or people. It can also be a one-time traumatic event that is left unresolved. Emotional abuse is an intentional assault by one person on another to so distort the victim's view of self that the victim allows the abuser to control him or her.

I conclude this book and this discussion of toxic people with the most important point of all: You deserve to be treated with respect, honor, and dignity at all times, by all people. It's true that each of us encounters difficult individuals and must endure offensive actions from selfish people on occasion. That is a part of life, but …

- Ongoing disrespect is unacceptable;

- Consistent unkindness is not justified; and

- Injustice of any kind should never be tolerated.

If a toxic person is turning your life into a toxic experience, that is not what God intends for you. Be courageous. Be strong. Be persistent. Be resilient. And be free of toxic people.

Notes

1   Diane Mapes, "Toxic friends? 8 in 10 people endure poisonous pals," *Today Show*. August 22, 2011. *https://www.today.com/health/toxic-friends-8-10-people-endure-poisonous-pals-1C9413205*.

2   Abigail Brenner, "Toxic People," *Psychology Today*. September 24, 2016.

3   Travis Bradberry, "10 Toxic People You Should Avoid At All Costs," *Forbes*. November 10, 2015.

4   Lisa Mooney, "How Does Pessimism Affect the Workplace?" azcentral USA Today Network. *https://yourbusiness.azcentral.com/significant-tardiness-work-6604.html*.

5   Abigail Brenner, "8 Traits the Most Toxic People in Your Life Share," *Psychology Today*. August 29, 2016.

6   Bradberry, "10 Toxic People."

7   Brenner, "8 Traits of the Most Toxic People."

8   Vanessa Van Edwards, "The 7 Types of Toxic People and How to Spot Them," *Science of People.* *https://www.scienceofpeople.com/toxic-people.*

9   Philip Yancey, *What's So Amazing About Grace?* (Zondervan, 1997), 71.

10 Yancey, *What's So Amazing About Grace?* 180.

For Further Reading

Books on Related Topics by Dr. Gregory L. Jantz

Controlling Your Anger Before It Controls You: A Guide for Women (Revell, 2013)

Don't Call It Love: Breaking the Cycle of Relationship Dependency; co-authored by Dr. Tim Clinton (Revell, 2015)

Happy for the Rest of Your Life: Four Steps to Contentment, Hope, and Joy - and the three keys to staying there (Siloam, 2009)

Healing Depression for Life: The Personalized Approach That Offers New Hope for Lasting Relief (Tyndale, 2019)

Healing the Scars of Addiction: Reclaiming Your Life and Moving Into a Healthy Future (Revell, 2018).

Healing the Scars of Childhood Abuse: Moving Beyond the Past Into a Healthy Future (Revell, 2017)

Healing the Scars of Emotional Abuse, Revised and Updated Edition (Revell, 2009)

How to De-Stress Your Life (Revell, 2008)

Overcoming Anxiety, Worry, and Fear (Revell, 2011)

Rebuilding Trust After Betrayal: Hope and Help for Broken Relationships (Aspire Press, 2021)

The Anxiety Reset: A Life-Changing Approach to Overcoming Fear, Stress, Worry, Panic Attacks, OCD, and More (Tyndale, 2021)

When a Loved One Is Addicted: How to Offer Hope and Help (Aspire Press, 2021)

Image Credits

MORE RESOURCES FROM DR. GREGORY L. JANTZ

Unmasking Emotional Abuse

Six Steps to Reduce Stress

Ten Tips for Parenting the Smartphone Generation

Five Keys to Dealing with Depression

Seven Answers for Anxiety

Five Keys to Raising Boys

Five Keys to Health and Healing

40 Answers for Teens' Top Questions

When a Loved One Is Addicted

Social Media and Depression

Rebuilding Trust after Betrayal

How to Deal with Toxic People

www.hendricksonrose.com